West Coast Covered Bridges
by
Harold Stiver

Copyright Statement

West Coast Covered Bridges

A Guide for Photographers and Explorers

Table of Contents

How to use this Book

For each of the 63 historical or Traditional Covered Bridges remaining in California, Oregon and Washington states, We have included photographs as well as descriptive and statistical data. Traditional Covered Bridges are those that follow the building practices of the Nineteenth Century and the early part of the Twentieth Century or those built later that follow those methods. All of these bridges have had repairs done as portions wear out, and some may have been almost entirely replaced through the years. I have used "The National Society for the Preservation of Covered Bridges, Inc." list of what they consider as Traditional Bridges.

Following is data included for each bridge

Name: This is listed in bold type, and where there are other names, it is the common name or the name listed on an accompanying plaque.

Other Names: Underneath the Common Name in brackets, you will find other names that the bridge has been known by.

Nearest County and Township are listed.

It is frustrating to go on an excursion to see something and not be able to find it. This book offers you multiple ways to ensure that doesn't happen.

GPS Position: This is our recommended method. Enter the coordinates in a good GPS unit and it should take you right there. You, of course, must use care that you are not led off road or on a dangerous route.

Detailed Driving Directions: Directions from a town near to the bridge.

Builder: If known, the name of the original builder(s) is listed.

Year Built: As well as the year built, if it has been moved it will shown with the year preceded by the letter M and, if a major repair has been done, the year will be shown preceded by the letter R.

Truss Type: The type for the particular bridge will be listed. If you are interested in more information on the various types of trusses, access "Truss Types" from the Table of Contents.

Dimensions: The length and number of spans

Photo Tips: The compass orientation is given which gives the user some indication of the sun position. if there are superior setup positions or other composition elements, they may be noted. You may also find some useful ideas from reading "Photographing Covered Bridges" from the Table of Contents.

Notes: A place where you can find additional items of interest about the bridge.

World Index Number:
Covered bridges are assigned a number to keep track of them which consists of three numbers separated by hyphens.

The first number represents the number of the U.S. State in alphabetical order. Following number 50 for the 50th state are additional numbers for Canadian provinces. Thus the numbers 05 represents California.

The second set of numbers represents the county of that state, again based on alphabetical order. Humboldt is the 12th county alphabetically in California, and it is designated as 05-12.

Each bridge in that county is given a number as it was discovered or built. Zane's Ranch was the fifth bridge discovered or built in the County of Humboldt, California and it therefore has the designation of 05-12-05. Sometimes you will see the first set of numbers replaced by the abbreviation for the state, thus CA-12-05.

A bridge is sometimes substantially rebuilt or replaced and it then has the suffix #2 added to it.

National Register of Historic Places: If the bridge has registered, the date is given.

Photographing Covered Bridges

Some standard positions

Portal: Taken to show the ends of bridge or bridge opening. This view, usually symmetrical, will include various signs posted. This is also a good way to get run over, so be careful!

3/4 view: Shows both the front and sides of the bridge, and is often the most attractive.

Side view: Taken from a bank or from the river, this gives not only a nice view of the bridge but usually allows for some interesting foreground elements.

Interior view: An image taken from the interior of the bridge will show some interesting structure but there is not a lot of available light. A tripod is important and HDR processing is helpful.

Landscape View: With the bridge smaller in the frame, you can introduce the habitat around it, particularly effective with colorful autumn foliage.

Using HDR(High Dynamic Range)

HDR is a process where multiple images of varying exposure are combined to make one image.

It has a bad name with some people because many HDR images are super-saturated, a kind of digital age version of an Elvis painted on velvet. However, the process is actually about getting a full range of exposure with no burnt out highlights or blocked shadows. This is an ideal processing solution for photographing Covered Bridges where you often have open light sky set against dark shadowed landscape and structure.

I use a series of three exposures at levels of -1 2/3, 0, +1 2/3, and this normally runs the full exposure range encountered. It is important to use a stable tripod.

One situation where you may need a larger series is shooting from within a bridge and using the window to frame an outside scene. The dynamic range is huge and you will need to have a series with a much larger range.

There are a number of software programs you can use to combine these images including newer editions of Photoshop. I use Photomatix which I have found very versatile and easy to use.

Best times for photographing bridges
Mornings and evenings are generally the best times for outdoor photography but the use of HDR processing makes it easier even in bright direct light. Although any season is good for bridge photography including the winter, fall foliage included in a scene can be spectacular.

A Short History of Covered Bridges

Let's deal with that often posed question; "Why were the bridges covered"

1. Crossing animals thought it was a barn and entered easily. I like this suggestion, it shows imagination. However, its not the answer although the original bridges normally had no windows and this is said to be because animals would not be spooked by the sight of the water.

2. To cover up the unsightly truss structure. I don't think those early pioneers were that sensitive, and personally, I like the look of the trusses.

3. To keep snow off the travelled portion. In fact the bridge owners often paid to have the insides "snowed" in order to facilitate sleighs.

4. It offered some privacy to courting couples, hence "kissing bridges". That is a nice romantic notion but no.

In fact, the bridge was covered for economic reasons. The truss system was where much of the bridge's cost was found, and if left open to the elements, it deteriorated and the bridge became unstable and unsafe. Covering it protected this valuable portion and the roof could be replaced as needed with inexpensive materials and unskilled labour. Without coverings, a bridge might only have a life span of a decade while one that was covered often lasted 75 years or more before repairs became necessary. Besides extending the longevity of a bridge, wooden covered bridges had the virtue that they could be constructed of local materials and there were many available workers skilled in working with wood.

The first known Covered Bridge in North America was built in 1804 by Theodore Burr. It was called the Waterford bridge and it spanned the Hudson River in New York.

For the rest of the century and into the 20th Century, Covered bridge building boomed as the country became populated and people needed to travel between communities. The cost of constructing and maintaining a bridge was normally borne by the nearby community and many bridges charged a toll as a method of offsetting these costs.

The period from 1825 to 1875 was the heyday of bridge building but near the end of that period iron bridges began to supplant them.

The number of Covered bridges may have numbered 10,000 but have now dropped to about 840 spread throughout North America. Many have Historical Designations which provides them protection and many communities are interested in protecting their local historical bridges.

Berta's Ranch Covered Bridge
County: Humboldt, California
Township: Eureka

GPS Position: 40°43'28"N 124°10'37"W
Directions: From Ridgewood Heights go west on Ridgewood Dr for 1.2 mi and turn left onto Elk River Rd. After 0.9 mi turn right onto Bertas Rd where you find the bridge
Crosses: Elk River
Carries: Bertras Road (By-passed)

Builder: Not known
Year Built: 1936
Truss Type: Queen
Dimensions: 1 span, 52 feet

Photo Tip: Easy from all sides with good portal view
Notes: The bridge is unpainted and features long approach ramps. It has the same length and appearance as nearby Zane's Ranch which was opened a year later

World Index Number: CA/05-12-02
National Register of Historic Places: Not listed

Zane's Ranch Covered Bridge
County: Humboldt, California
Township: Eureka

GPS Position: 40°43'4"N 124°10'8"W
Directions: From Ridgewood go west on Walnut Dr and continue for 1.3 mi. Turn left onto Elk River Rd and in 1.6 mi turn right onto Zanes Rd where the bridge is a short way.
Crosses: Elk River
Carries: Zanes Road

Builder: Not known
Year Built: 1937 (R2018)
Truss Type: Queen
Dimensions:1 span, 52 feet

Photo Tip: Easy all sides including a good portal view with approaches
Notes: Similar to Berta's Ranch and may be the same builder

World Index Number: CA/05-12-05
National Register of Historic Places: Not listed

Brookwood Covered Bridge

County: Humboldt, California
Township: Arcata

GPS Position: 40°49'55"N 124°2'44"W
Directions: From Jacoby Creek, head southeast on Brookwood Dr for 0.1 miles and find the bridge
Crosses: Jacoby Creek
Carries: Brookwood Dr.

Builder: Earl Biehn
Year Built: 1969 (R2013)
Truss Type: Howe
Dimensions: 1 span, 66 feet

Photo Tip: Sides are obstructed but a good portal view
Notes: In 2013, the county discussed replacing the structure with a modern bridge. Local pressure changed their minds and the structure was repaired.

World Index Number: CA/05-12-05
National Register of Historic Places: Not listed

Wawona Covered Bridge
County: Mariposa, California
Township: Wawona

GPS Position: 37°32'19"N 119°39'17"W
Directions: From South Wawona, head southwest on Forest Dr for 0.7 mi where you find the bridge
Crosses: South Fork Merced River
Carries: Forest Drive

Builder: Galen Clark
Year Built: 1868 (R1937) (1955)
Truss Type: Queen
Dimensions: 1 span, 66 feet

Photo Tip: There are excellent river level side views
Notes: It is now an exhibit at Pioneer Yosemite History Center

World Index Number: CA/05-22-01
National Register of Historic Places: January 11, 2007

Bridgeport Covered Bridge
County: Nevada, California
Township: Nevada City

GPS Position: 39°17'33"N 121°11'42"W
Directions: From the town of French Corral, head NW on Pleasant Valley Rd for 2.7 mi and the bridge is on the left
Crosses: South Fork Yuba River
Carries: Bridgeport Covered Bridge Road

Builder: J.W. Woods
Year Built: 1862
Truss Type: Howe and Arch
Dimensions: 1 span, 226 feet

Photo Tip: Excellent side views are available
Notes: The bridge was by-passed in 1972. It is the second longest single span covered bridge in the United States

World Index Number: CA/05-29-01
National Register of Historic Places: 1971

Felton Covered Bridge

County: Santa Cruz, California
Township: Felton

GPS Position: 37°03'03"N 122°04'15"W
Directions: From Felton, take Graham Hill Rd southeast from CA-9 for 0.2 mi and turn right onto Covered Bridge Rd S for 0.1 mi where you find the bridge
Crosses: San Lorenzo River
Carries: Covered Bridge Rd

Builder: Cotton Brothers
Year Built: 1892 (R1987)
Truss Type: Modified Pratt
Dimensions: 1 span, 163 feet

Photo Tip: Good portal views, sides available with care
Notes: The bridge was closed and by-passed in 1938. It underwent a major restoration in 1987

World Index Number: CA/05-44-02
National Register of Historic Places: 1973

Powder Works CB (Paradise Park, Masonic Park)
County: Santa Cruz, California
Township: Santa Cruz

GPS Position: 37°0'38"N 122°2'38"W
Directions: From Paradise Park, head north on Keystone Way for 0.6 mi and after 0.4 mi, turn right to stay on Keystone Way and the bridge is on the left
Crosses: San Lorenzo River
Carries: Keystone Way
Builder: California Powder Works
Year Built: 1872
Truss Type: Smith Triple
Dimensions: 1+ span, 180 feet

Photo Tip: Easy from all sides
Notes: In 1872, California Powder Works built the bridge to service their black powder mill. After the mill closed, it continued in use by nearby residents

World Index Number: CA/05-44-03
National Register of Historic Places: April 15, 2015

Knight's Ferry Covered Bridge
County: Stanislaus, California
Township: Knight's Ferry

GPS Position: 37°49'10.7"N 120°39'49.4"W
Directions: From Knight's Ferry, head east off Sonora Road on Covered Bridge Rd and the bridge is 0.1 mi
Crosses: Stanislaus River
Carries: Covered Bridge Rd (By-passed)

Builder: Schuylkill Bridge Company
Year Built: 1864
Truss Type: Howe
Dimensions: 3+ spans, 330 feet

Photo Tip: Great 3/4 and side views
Notes: This bridge was built to replace a ferry at this spot. It is the second-longest covered bridge in the United States

World Index Number: CA/05-50-01
National Register of Historic Places: October 16, 2012

Oregon Creek Covered Bridge
County: Yuba, California
Township: Log Cabin

GPS Position: 39°23'48"N 121°4'52"W
Directions: From North San Juan, head NW on CA-49 N for 2.8 mi and turn right onto Alleghany Rd. The bridge is on the right in 0.3 mi
Crosses: Oregon Creek
Carries: Alleghany Rd

Builder: Thomas Freeman
Year Built: 1880 (R2018)
Truss Type: Queen
Dimensions: 1 span, 105 feet

Photo Tip: Easy from all sides including good 3/4 view
Notes: The bridge received extensive repairs in 2018 including the roof and abutments

World Index Number: CA/05-58-01
National Register of Historic Places: Not listed

California County Map

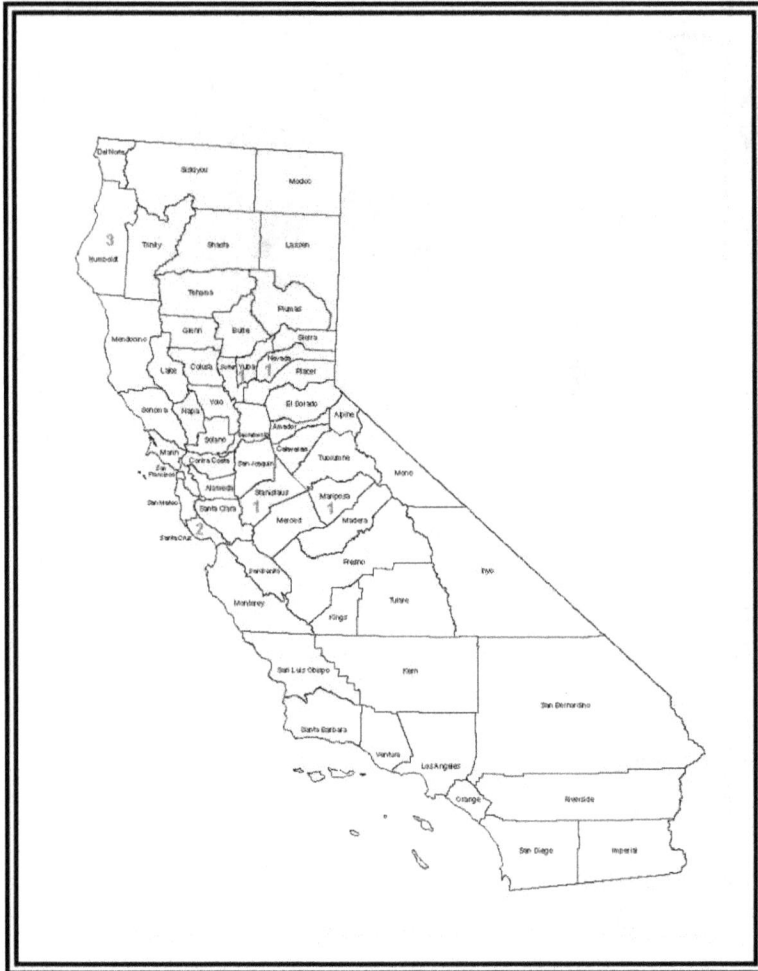

Humboldt County Bridge Tour

California Covered bridges tend to be very spread out and this makes it unrealistic to plan a driving tour that includes a lot of bridges.

However, Humboldt County has three bridges that can take only 30 minutes driving to visit all three. The following order is an efficient plan to accomplish this. You can reverse the order if it is convenient.

Brookwood Covered Bridge   40°49'55"N 124°2'44"W
Berta's Ranch Covered Bridge 40°43'28"N 124°10'37"W
Zane's Ranch Covered Bridge 40°43'4"N 124°10'8"W

Harris Covered Bridge
County: Benton, Oregon
Township: Wren

GPS Position: 44°34'48.0"N 123°27'36.7"W
Directions: From Wren, head west on Echo Hills Rd for 0.4 mi and turn right onto Wren Rd. After 0.1 mi turn left onto Harris Rd and the bridge is 2.5 mi.
Crosses: Mary's River
Carries: Harris Road
Builder: H. W. Fiedler
Year Built: 1936
Truss Type: Howe
Dimensions: 1 span, 75 feet

Photo Tip: All sides but pick side setup carefully
Notes: Harris Covered Bridge was named for George Harris, an early settler. Some sources say it was built in 1929.

World Index Number: OR/37-02-04
National Register of Historic Places: November 29, 1979

Hayden Covered Bridge
County: Benton, Oregon
Township: Alsea

GPS Position: 44°22'59.2"N 123°37'50.5"W
Directions: From Alsea, head west on OR-34 W/E Main St for 1.8 mi and turn left onto Hayden Rd where the bridge is 0.1 mi
Crosses: Alsea River
Carries: Hayden Rd
Builder: Not known
Year Built: 1945
Truss Type: Howe
Dimensions: 1 span, 91 feet

Photo Tip: Nice 3/4 and portal views
Notes: A Covered Bridge was built at this site in 1918. In 1945 it was replaced by the current bridge after the original was deemed to be unsafe.

World Index Number: OR/37-02-05#2
National Register of Historic Places: Not Listed

Irish Bend Covered Bridge
County: Benton, Oregon
Township: Corvallis

GPS Position: 44°33'59.5"N 123°18'02.9"W
Directions: From Corvallis, head south on SW 4th St toward SW Madison Ave for 0.5 mi and keep right to continue on US-20 W. In 1.3 mi turn right onto SW 35th St and in 0.8 mi turn left onto SW Campus Way where the bridge is 0.5 mi
Crosses: Oak Creek
Carries: SW Campus Way
Builder: Benton County workforce
Year Built: 1954 (M1989)
Truss Type: Howe
Dimensions: 1 span, 60 feet
Photo Tip: Easy from all sides
Notes: After being bypassed, it was relocated to the Oregon State University campus in1989.

World Index Number: OR/37-02-09#2
National Register of Historic Places: March 27, 2013

Sandy Creek Covered Bridge
County: Coos, Oregon
Township: Remote

GPS Position: 43°00'22.9"N 123°53'30.4"W
Directions: Head northeast from OR-42 on Sandy Creek Rd for 200 feet and the bridge is on the left
Crosses: Sandy Creek
Carries: N/A

Builder: A. Guthrie & Company
Year Built: 1921
Truss Type: Howe
Dimensions: 1 span, 60 feet

Photo Tip: Easy from all sides
Notes: In late 1981, the local Lions Club organized developing the site as a public park with picnic tables in the bridge.

World Index Number: OR/37-06-09
National Register of Historic Places: November 29, 1979

Pass Creek Covered Bridge
County: Douglas, Oregon
Township: Drain

GPS Position: 43°39'38.3"N 123°18'59.7"W
Directions: 101 W A Ave, Drain
Crosses: Pass Creek
Carries: Pedestrian Walkway

Builder: Not known
Year Built: 1925 (M1987) (R19169)
Truss Type: Howe
Dimensions: 1 span, 61 feet

Photo Tip: Portal may be the only unobstructed exterior view
Notes: The bridge was moved in 1987 to its present location and acts as a Pedestrian Walkway

World Index Number: OR/37-10-02
National Register of Historic Places: Not listed

Rochester Covered Bridge
County: Douglas, Oregon
Township: Sutherlin

GPS Position: 43°39'38.3"N 123°18'59.7"W
Directions: 101 W A Ave, Drain
Crosses: Pass Creek
Carries: Pedestrian Walkway

Builder: Not known
Year Built: 1925 (M1987) (R19169)
Truss Type: Howe
Dimensions: 1 span, 61 feet

Photo Tip: Portal may be the only unobstructed exterior view
Notes: The bridge was moved in 1987 to its present location and acts as a Pedestrian Walkway

World Index Number: OR/37-10-02
National Register of Historic Places: Not listed

Cavitt Creek Covered Bridge
County: Douglas, Oregon
Township: Glide

GPS Position: 43°14'38.8"N 123°01'18.4"W
Directions: From Peel, head south on Little River Rd for 1.2 mi and turn right onto Cavitt Creek Rd where you find the bridge
Crosses: Little River
Carries: Cavitt Creek Rd
Builder: Floyd C. Frear
Year Built: 1943
Truss Type: Howe
Dimensions: 1 span, 70 feet

Photo Tip: Sides need careful setup but other views good
Notes: The bridge is named for Robert L. Cavitt, an early settler who lived nearby.

World Index Number: OR/37-10-06
National Register of Historic Places: Not listed

Neal Lane Covered Bridge
County: Douglas, Oregon
Township: Myrtle Creek

GPS Position: 43°01'01.1"N 123°16'28.3"W
Directions: In Myrtle Creek, head east on E Riverside Dr for 0.2 mi and turn right onto Days Creek Cutoff Rd. After 0.7 mi turn left onto SE Neal Ln where you find the bridge

Crosses: Myrtle Creek
Carries: Neal Lane
Builder: Not known
Year Built: 1929
Truss Type: King
Dimensions: 1 span, 42 feet

Photo Tip: Easy from all sides
Notes: This is the only Oregon Covered Bridge which uses a Kingpost truss

World Index Number: OR/37-10-07
National Register of Historic Places: Not listed

Horse Creek Covered Bridge
County: Douglas, Oregon
Township: Myrtle Creek

GPS Position: 43°01'24.1"N 123°17'24.1"W
Directions: In Myrtle Creek, head east on N Main St from I-5 for 0.6 mi where you will find the bridge
Crosses: Myrtle Creek
Carries: Pedestrian Walkway

Builder: Not known
Year Built: 1930 (R1990) (M1990)
Truss Type: Howe
Dimensions: 1 span, 105 feet

Photo Tip: Good 3/4 view
Notes: The bridge was closed and bypassed in 1968. In 1990 it was moved to Myrtle Creek's Millsite Park

World Index Number: OR/37-10-14
National Register of Historic Places: Not listed

Antelope Creek Covered Bridge

County: Jackson, Oregon
Township: Eagle Point

GPS Position: 42°28'19.5"N 122°48'00.8"W
Directions: 104 N Royal Ave, Eagle Point
Crosses: Little Butte Creek
Carries: Pedestrian Walkway

Builder: Wes and Lyle Hartman
Year Built: 1922 (M1987)
Truss Type: Queen
Dimensions: 1 span, 58 feet

Photo Tip: A side view is available from the new bridge
Notes: In 1987 the bridge was moved from the nearby town of Medford to its present location in Eagle Point. It is now a pedestrian walkway in Covered Bridge Park

World Index Number: OR/37-15-02
National Register of Historic Places: 2012

Lost Creek Covered Bridge
County: Jackson, Oregon
Township: Lake Creek

GPS Position: 42°22'48.5"N 122°34'46.2"W
Directions: From Lakecreek, head south on S Fork Little Butte Creek Rd for 3.5 mi and turn right onto Lost Creek Rd where the bridge is 0.5 mi
Crosses: Lost Creek
Carries: Lost Creek Road
Builder: Not known
Year Built: 1881 or 1919
Truss Type: Queen
Dimensions: 1 span, 39 feet

Photo Tip: Easy from all sides
Notes: This is the shortest Covered Bridge in Oregon. Various sources disagree on the build date.

World Index Number: OR/37-15-03
National Register of Historic Places: November 29, 1979

Wimer Covered Bridge
County: Jackson, Oregon
Township: Wimer

GPS Position: 42°32'17.5"N 123°08'59.2"W
Directions: 838-878 Covered Bridge Rd, Wimer
Crosses: Evans Creek
Carries: Covered Bridge Rd

Builder: Not known
Year Built: 2008
Truss Type: Multiple King
Dimensions: 1 span, 85 feet

Photo Tip: Excellent portal view. Other views easy
Notes: The original covered bridge at this site was built in 1892. It collapsed in 2003 and was replaced with the present structure.

World Index Number: OR/37-15-05#2
National Register of Historic Places: Not listed

McKee Covered Bridge
County: Jackson, Oregon
Township: Ruch

GPS Position: 42°07'32.9"N 123°04'21.4"W
Directions: From Buncom, head NW on Little Applegate Rd for 2.9 mi and turn left onto Upper Applegate Rd. After 6.3 mi, turn left onto Eastside Rd and in 0.4 mi, continue onto McKee Bridge Road to find the bridge
Crosses: Applegate River
Carries: McKee Bridge Road
Builder: Jason Hartman and his son Wesley
Year Built: 1917 (R1985)
Truss Type: Howe
Dimensions: 1 span, 112 feet
Photo Tip: Open but sides need care to set up
Notes: The bridge was closed to vehicles in 1956. It is currently maintained by volunteers

World Index Number: OR/37-15-06
National Register of Historic Places: November 29, 1979

Grave Creek Covered Bridge (Sunny Valley)
County: Josephine, Oregon
Township: Sunny Valley

GPS Position: 42°38'10.0"N 123°22'39.5"W
Directions: From Sunny Valley, head south on Sunny Valley Loop for 0.2 mi to find the bridge
Crosses: Grave Creek
Carries: Sunny Valley Loop

Builder: J. Elmer Nelson
Year Built: 1920 (R2000)
Truss Type: Howe
Dimensions: 1 span, 105 feet

Photo Tip: The fenced approaches offer a good portal view
Notes: The rehabilitation in 2000 has the bridge in beautiful shape. It re-opened to traffic in 2001.

World Index Number: OR/37-17-01
National Register of Historic Places: November 29, 1979

Coyote Creek Covered Bridge (Swing Log)
County: Lane, Oregon
Township: Crow

GPS Position: 43°58'12.4"N 123°19'08.3"W
Directions: From Crow, head south on Territorial Hwy for 1.9 mi and turn right onto Coyote Creek Rd, the bridge is 0.1 mi
Crosses: Coyote Creek
Carries: Coyote Creek Road

Builder: Lane County workforce
Year Built: 1922 (R1970) (R2003)
Truss Type: Howe
Dimensions: 1 span, 60 feet

Photo Tip: The 3/4 view with fenced approaches is excellent
Notes: The 1970 repairs were needed when the roof collapsed due to snow load

World Index Number: OR/37-20-02
National Register of Historic Places: November 29, 1979

Wildcat Creek Covered Bridge (Austa)
County: Lane, Oregon
Township: Richardson

GPS Position: 44°00'10.9"N 123°39'18.2"W
Directions: From Linslaw, head east on Old Stagecoach Rd/ Richardson Upriver Rd for 2.2 mi and turn right onto Austa Rd/ Siuslaw Rd to find the bridge
Crosses: Wildcat Creek
Carries: Austa Road
Builder: Lane County workforce
Year Built: 1925
Truss Type: Howe
Dimensions: 1 span, 75 feet
Photo Tip: Portal views have nice treed background
Notes: When the bridge was constructed in 1925, it was an important passage to the coast. While it was bypassed for this, it remains active locally

World Index Number: OR/37-20-04
National Register of Historic Places: November 29, 1979

Lake Creek Covered Bridge (Nelson Mountain)
County: Lane, Oregon
Township: Greenleaf

GPS Position: 44°06'15.6"N 123°40'25.1"W
Directions: From Deadwood, head east on OR-36 E for 4.7 mi
and turn right onto Nelson Mountain Rd where the bridge is a
short distance
Crosses: Lake Creek
Carries: Nelson Mountain Rd
Builder: Lane County workforce
Year Built: 1928 (R1984
Truss Type: Howe
Dimensions: 1 span, 105 feet
Photo Tip: All sides are good especially 3/4 view
Notes: The 1984 rehabilitation replaced the wooden flooring
with concrete slab decking which was lowered into place by a
crane

World Index Number: OR/37-20-06
National Register of Historic Places: March 18, 1980

Goodpasture Covered Bridge
County: Lane, Oregon
Township: Vida

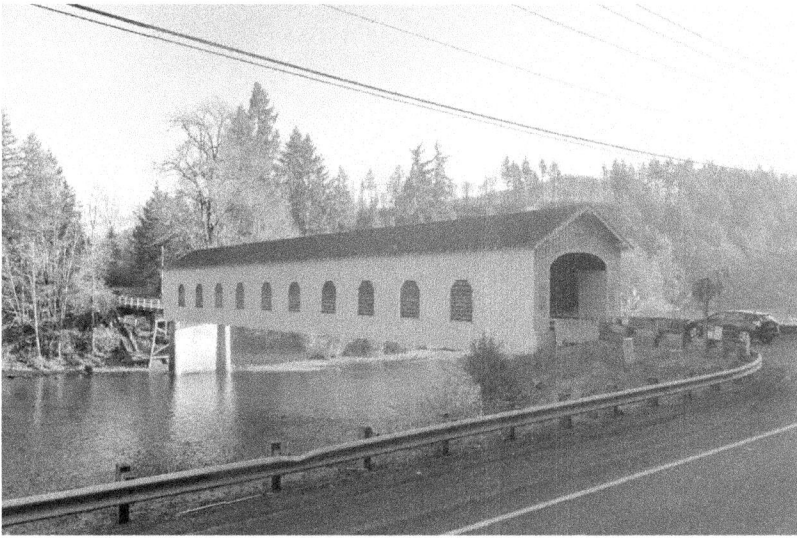

GPS Position: 44°08'53.0"N 122°35'15.0"W
Directions: From Vida, head NW on OR-126 W for 0.8 mi and turn left onto Goodpasture Rd to find the bridge
Crosses: McKenzie River
Carries: Goodpasture Road

Builder: Lane County workforce
Year Built: 1938 (R1942) (R1987)
Truss Type: Howe
Dimensions: 1 span, 165 feet

Photo Tip: Excellent easy views from all sides
Notes: The 1942 repairs were needed after a flood swept it off it's abutments.

World Index Number: OR/37-20-10
National Register of Historic Places: March 18, 1980

Belknap Covered Bridge (McKenzie River)
County: Lane, Oregon
Township: Rainbow

GPS Position: 44°10'04.9"N 122°13'42.1"W
Directions: From Rainbow, head east on McKenzie River Dr for 0.4 mi and turn right onto Belknap Bridge Road to find the bridge
Crosses: McKenzie River
Carries: Belknap Bridge Road
Builder: Lane County workforce
Year Built: 1965
Truss Type: Howe
Dimensions: 1 span, 120 feet

Photo Tip: The road curve in front gives a nice composition
Notes: This is the 4th covered bridge here. The current replaced a bridge destroyed in a 1964 flood

World Index Number: OR/37-20-11#4
National Register of Historic Places: November 29, 1979

Pengra Covered Bridge
County: Lane, Oregon
Township: Jasper

GPS Position: 43°57'57.9"N 122°50'42.8"W
Directions: From Jasper, head SW on Jasper Rd/Jasper Lowell Rd for 3.9 mi and turn left to stay on Jasper Lowell Rd for 0.2 mi. Turn right onto Place Rd and see the bridge
Crosses: Fall Creek
Carries: Place Rd
Builder: Lane County workforce
Year Built: 1938 (R1995) (R2015)
Truss Type: Howe
Dimensions: 1 span, 120 feet

Photo Tip: All easy with great portal view
Notes: The bridge was closed in 1979 and re-opened in 1995 after repairs where done. The roof was replaced in 2015.

World Index Number: OR/37-20-15#2
National Register of Historic Places: November 29, 1979

Unity Covered Bridge
County: Lane, Oregon
Township: Lowell

GPS Position: 43°56'42.5"N 122°46'32.3"W
Directions: From Unity, head south on Big Fall Creek Rd for 0.7 mi and turn right onto Jasper Lowell Rd to find the bridge
Crosses: Fall Creek
Carries: Jasper Lowell Rd
Builder: Lane County workforce
Year Built: 1936 (R1986) (R2014)
Truss Type: Howe
Dimensions: 1 span, 90 feet

Photo Tip: Sides need careful setup, nice portal view
Notes: The flooring, guard rails and exterior paint were repaired in 1986 and the roof in 2014

World Index Number: OR/37-20-17#2
National Register of Historic Places: November 29, 1979

Lowell Covered Bridge
County: Lane, Oregon
Township: Lowell

GPS Position: 43°54'34.5"N 122°46'46.3"W
Directions: From Dexter, head SW on OR-58 E for 1.6 mi and turn left onto S Pioneer St and see the bridge
Crosses: Dexter Reservoir, Middle Fork, Willamette River
Carries: Pioneer St
Builder: Lane County workforce
Year Built: 1945 (R2005)
Truss Type: Howe
Dimensions: 1 span, 165 feet

Photo Tip: Nice 3/4 view available
Notes: This bridge replaced the original 1907 bridge damaged by a truck. It was raised 5 feet when the as Dexter Reservoir was completed

World Index Number: OR/37-20-18#2
National Register of Historic Places: November 29, 1979

Parvin Covered Bridge
County: Lane, Oregon
Township: Dexter

GPS Position: 43°53'58.1"N 122°49'22.9"W
Directions: From Dexter, head south on Lost Creek Rd for 0.5 mi and turn right onto Parvin Rd where the bridge is 0.8 mi
Crosses: Lost Creek
Carries: Parvin Rd

Builder: George W. Breeding
Year Built: 1921
Truss Type: Howe
Dimensions: 1 span, 75 feet

Photo Tip: Easy setups from all sides
Notes: The bridge was bypassed in the 1970s but after the 1986 rehabilitation it was reopened.

World Index Number: OR/37-20-19#2
National Register of Historic Places: November 29, 1979

Currin Covered Bridge
County: Lane, Oregon
Township: Cottage Grove

GPS Position: 43°47'34.9"N 122°59'47.3"W
Directions: From Cottage Grove, head SW on Row River Rd/ Row River Cutoff Rd for 2.9 mi and turn right onto Layng Rd and the bridge
Crosses: Row River
Carries: Laying Road
Builder: Lane County workforce
Year Built: 1925 (R1995)
Truss Type: Howe
Dimensions: 1 span, 105 feet

Photo Tip: Side view from the new bridge
Notes: This bridge is unusual for Oregon covered bridges in that it is primarily painted red rather than white

World Index Number: OR/37-20-22#2
National Register of Historic Places: November 29, 1979

Dorena Covered Bridge (Star)
County: Lane, Oregon
Township: Dorena

GPS Position: 43°44'15.4"N 122°53'01.3"W
Directions: From Dorena, head north on Row River Rd for 1.9 mi and continue straight onto Government Rd/Shoreview Dr and the bridge
Crosses: Row River
Carries: Government Rd/Shoreview Dr
Builder: Lane County workforce
Year Built: 1949 (R1996)
Truss Type: Howe
Dimensions: 1 span, 105 feet

Photo Tip: Side view from the new bridge
Notes: Built after the Dorena Dam was built, it was bypassed in 1974

World Index Number: OR/37-20-23#2
National Register of Historic Places: November 29, 1979

Moseby Creek Covered Bridge
County: Lane, Oregon
Township: Cottage Grove

GPS Position: 43°46'41.4"N 123°00'17.3"W
Directions: From Walden, head northeast on Layng Rd for 0.2 mi to the bridge
Crosses: Moseby Creek
Carries: laying Road

Builder: Lane County workforce
Year Built: 1920 (R1990) (R2002)
Truss Type: Howe
Dimensions: 1 span, 90 feet

Photo Tip: Good portal and 3/4 setups
Notes: The Mosby Creek Covered Bridge is the only area covered bridge still open to traffic

World Index Number: OR/37-20-27
National Register of Historic Places: November 29, 1979

Stewart Covered Bridge
County: Lane, Oregon
Township: Cottage Grove

GPS Position: 43°45'57.6"N 122°59'38.9"W
Directions: From Walden, head southeast on Mosby Creek Rd for 1.1 mi and turn left onto Garoutte Rd for the bridge
Crosses: Mosby Creek
Carries: Garoutte Road

Builder: Lane County workforce
Year Built: 1930   (R1969)
Truss Type: Howe
Dimensions: 1 span, 60 feet

Photo Tip: Easy from all sides
Notes: In 1969, the roof collapsed from a heavy snow load. The structure was bypassed in the 1990s.

World Index Number: OR/37-20-28
National Register of Historic Places: November 29, 1979

Earnest Covered Bridge (Russell)
County: Lane, Oregon
Township: Marcola

GPS Position: 44°12'05.5"N 122°50'11.3"W
Directions: From Mabel, head SW on Marcola Rd for 1.1 mi
and turn left onto Paschelke Rd and the bridge
Crosses: Mowawk River
Carries: Paschelke Road
Builder: Lane County workforce
Year Built: 1938
Truss Type: Howe
Dimensions: 1 span, 75 feet

Photo Tip: Portal view with approaches is available
Notes: The bridge replaced the original covered bridge at this
location called the Adams Covered Bridge built by A.N. Striker
in 1903

World Index Number: OR/37-20-35#2
National Register of Historic Places: November 29, 1979

Wendling Covered Bridge
County: Lane, Oregon
Township: Marcola

GPS Position: 44°11'28.8"N 122°47'55.6"W
Directions: In Wendling, go north on Wendling Rd and the bridge is a short ditance
Crosses: Mill Creek
Carries: Wendling Road

Builder: Lane County workforce
Year Built: 1938
Truss Type: Howe
Dimensions: 1 span, 60 feet

Photo Tip: Available at all sides, side setups need care
Notes: At one time the Wendling Covered Bridge's interior was covered with circus posters, unfortunately gone now

World Index Number: OR/37-20-36
National Register of Historic Places: November 29, 1979

Deadwood Creek Covered Bridge
County: Lane, Oregon
Township: Greenleaf

GPS Position: 44°08'36.9"N 123°43'13.5"W
Directions: From Deadwood, head NE on Deadwood Creek
Rd for 5.0 mi and turn right onto Deadwood Loop Rd and the
bridge is 0.3 mi
Crosses: Deadwood Creek
Carries: Deadwood Loop Road
Builder: Miller Sorenson
Year Built: 1932 (R1986)
Truss Type: Howe
Dimensions: 1 span, 105 feeet

Photo Tip: Excellent in all sides
Notes: The bridge was bypassed in the 1970s. Lane County
workers rehabilitated it in 1986

World Index Number: OR/37-20-38
National Register of Historic Places: November 29, 1979

Office Covered Bridge
County: Lane, Oregon
Township: Westfir

GPS Position: 43°45'30.5"N 122°29'44.6"W
Directions: From the town of Westfir, take Westoak Rd off
Wesrfir Rd where the bridge is a short way
Crosses: North Fork of the Willamette River
Carries: Westoak Rd

Builder: Westfir Lumber Company
Year Built: 1944 (R1993) (R2002)
Truss Type: Howe
Dimensions: 1 span, 180 feet

Photo Tip: Easy portal and 3/4 views
Notes: The longest Covered Bridge in Oregon and the only
bridge west of the Mississippi River with a separate walkway

World Index Number: OR/37-20-39
National Register of Historic Places: November 29, 1979

Chambers Railroad Covered Bridge
County: Lane, Oregon
Township: Cottage Grove

GPS Position: 43°47'21.7"N 123°04'10.9"W
Directions: 1231 S River Rd, Cottage Grove
Crosses: Coast Fork of the Willamette River
Carries: River Road
Builder: J.H. Chambers Lumber Mill
Year Built: 2011
Truss Type: Howe
Dimensions: 1 span, 78 feet

Photo Tip: Nice portal view with steps in foreground
Notes: The Chambers Covered Railroad Bridge is the only surviving railroad bridge west of the Mississippi River. It is pedestrian only and built the same as the original 1925 bridge.

World Index Number: OR/37-20-40#2
National Register of Historic Places: Not listed

Centennial Covered Bridge
County: Lane, Oregon
Township: Cottage Grove

GPS Position: 43°47'50.8"N 123°03'51.9"W
Directions: In Cottage Grove, head east on E Main St from OR-99 for 0.3 mi and find the bridge
Crosses: Coast Fork of the Willamette River
Carries: E Main St

Builder: Volunteers
Year Built: 1987
Truss Type: Howe
Dimensions: 1 span, 84 feet

Photo Tip: Easy from all sides
Notes: The bridge is a 3/8 scale of the Chambers Bridge built for Cottage Grove's 100th anniversary

World Index Number: OR/37-20-41
National Register of Historic Places: Not listed

Chitwood Covered Bridge
County: Lincoln, Oregon
Township: Chitwood

GPS Position: 44°39'15.2"N 123°49'03.6"W
Directions: From Eddyville, head north on Crystal Crk Lp for 5.0 mi and turn left onto Chitwood Rd to find the bridge
Crosses: Yaquina River
Carries: Chitwood Road

Builder: Otis Hamar
Year Built: 1928 (R1984)
Truss Type: Howe
Dimensions: 1 span, 96 feet

Photo Tip: There is a portal view with nicely treed background
Notes: In 1984 there where plans to demolish the bridge but a federal grant provided the funds to rehabilitate it instead

World Index Number: OR/37-21-03
National Register of Historic Places: November 29, 1979

North Fork Yachats River Covered Bridge
County: Lincoln, Oregon
Township: Yachats

GPS Position: 44°18'36.0"N 123°58'11.0"W
Directions: From Yachats, head east on Yachats River Rd for 6.9 mi and turn left onto N Yachats River Rd where the bridge is 1.5 mi
Crosses: North Fork Yachats River
Carries: Yachats River Road
Builder: Otis Hamar
Year Built: 1938 (R1987)
Truss Type: Howe
Dimensions: 1 span, 42 feet

Photo Tip: Sides are obstructed but other views are good
Notes: One of the shortest covered bridges in Oregon, it is just 9 miles from the Pacific Ocean

World Index Number: OR/37-21-08
National Register of Historic Places: November 29, 1979

Fisher School Covered Bridge
County: Lincoln, Oregon
Township: Fisher

GPS Position: 44°17'29.9"N 123°50'29.0"W
Directions: From Fisher, head west on 5 Rivers/NF-32 for 0.1 mi and find the bridge
Crosses: Five Rivers
Carries: 5 Rivers Road

Builder: George Melvin
Year Built: 1919 (R2001)
Truss Type: Howe
Dimensions: 1 span, 72 feet

Photo Tip: Easy from all sides with a great 3/4 view
Notes: The bridge was rehabilitated in 2001 with the help of federal and county funds

World Index Number: OR/37-21-11
National Register of Historic Places: November 29, 1979

Fisher School Covered Bridge
County: Lincoln, Oregon
Township: Rose Lodge

GPS Position: 44°59'34.4"N 123°53'15.4"W
Directions: From OR-18 just south of Rose Lodge, head south on N Bear Creek Rd for 1.0 mi and the bridge
Crosses: Bear Creek
Carries: Bear Creek Road
Builder: Kerry Sweitz
Year Built: 1914 (M1997)
Truss Type: Howe
Dimensions: 1 span, 66 feet
Photo Tip: Easy all sides. Private, permission needed
Notes: The bridge was bypassed in the 1960s and by 1997 it was dismantled. The Sweitz family obtained the timbers and rebuilt on their property

World Index Number: OR/37-21-14
National Register of Historic Places: Listing removed 1998

Hannah Covered Bridge
County: Linn, Oregon
Township: Lyons

GPS Position: 44°42'43.4"N 122°43'06.3"W
Directions: From Jordan, head west on OR-226 W for 1.6 mi
and turn left onto Camp Morrison Dr and see the bridge
Crosses: Thomas Creek
Carries: Camp Morrison Dr
Builder: Linn County workforce
Year Built: 1936
Truss Type: Howe
Dimensions: 1 span, 105 feet

Photo Tip: Sides need careful setup, other views good
Notes: The bridge is named for John Joseph Hannah, an
early settler who built a sawmill in the area

World Index Number: OR/37-22-02
National Register of Historic Places: November 29, 1979

Shimanek Covered Bridge
County: Linn, Oregon
Township: Scio

GPS Position: 44°42'56.4"N 122°48'15.8"W
Directions: From Scio, head east on OR-226 E for 2.2 mi and turn left onto Richardson Gap Rd and the bridge is 0.7 mi
Crosses: Thomas Creek
Carries: Richardson Gap Road
Builder: Hamilton Construction Company
Year Built: 1966 (R2002)
Truss Type: Howe
Dimensions: 1 span, 130 feet

Photo Tip: Portal and approach fences are available
Notes: A flood caused damage in 1996 and Linn County workmen repaired it in 2002. The red paint is unusual for an Oregon Covered Bridge

World Index Number: OR/37-22-03#2
National Register of Historic Places: February 2, 1987

Gilkey Covered Bridge
County: Linn, Oregon
Township: Jefferson

GPS Position: 44°41'16.3"N 122°54'12.4"W
Directions: From Scio, head west on NW 1st Ave for 0.2 mi and continue onto Robinson Dr for 2.4 mi. Turn left onto Goar Rd and the bridge is 1.1 mi
Crosses: Thomas Creek
Carries: Goar Rd
Builder: Linn County workforce
Year Built: 1939 (R1998)
Truss Type: Howe
Dimensions: 1 span, 120 feet
Photo Tip: Easy from all sides
Notes: The 1998 repairs were the result of truck damage the previous year.

World Index Number: OR/37-22-04
National Register of Historic Places: February 19, 1987

Weddle Covered Bridge (Devaney)
County: Linn, Oregon
Township: Jefferson

GPS Position: 44°23'40.6"N 122°43'35.8"W
Directions: From Sweet Home, head south on 12th Ave for 0.1 mi and turn left onto Kalmia St, and then turn right onto 14th Ave. In 0.1 mi turn left to the bridge
Crosses: Ames Creek
Carries: Pedestrian walkway
Builder: Not known
Year Built: 1937 (M1987)
Truss Type: Howe
Dimensions: 1 span, 120 feet
Photo Tip: Easy and open all sides
Notes: The bridge originally spanned Thomas Creek. It was dismantled in 1987 and rebuilt at Sankey Park in Sweet Home in 1989.

World Index Number: OR/37-22-05#2
National Register of Historic Places: Delisted in 1989

Larwood Covered Bridge
County: Linn, Oregon
Township: Lacomb

GPS Position: 44°37'50.4"N 122°44'27.3"W
Directions: From Crabtree, head east on Fish Hatchery Dr and the bridge is 6.6 mi
Crosses: Crabtree Creek
Carries: Fish Hatchery Dr

Builder: Linn County workforce
Year Built: 1939 (R2002)
Truss Type: Howe
Dimensions: 1 span, 105 feet

Photo Tip: Sides are obstructed, other views are good
Notes: The open sides revealing the trusses are very attractive. The site is a popular place to swim

World Index Number: OR/37-22-06#2
National Register of Historic Places: November 29, 1979

Hoffman Covered Bridge
County: Linn. Oregon
Township: Crabtree

GPS Position: 44°39'12.0"N 122°53'25.5"W
Directions: From Crabtree, head north on Hungry Hill Rd for 1.6 mi to the bridge
Crosses: Crabtree Creek
Carries: Hungry Hill Road

Builder: Lee Hoffman
Year Built: 1936
Truss Type: Howe
Dimensions: 1 span, 90 feet

Photo Tip: Portal and 3/4 views are good
Notes: The bridge was named for the builder, Lee Hoffman

World Index Number: OR/37-22-08
National Register of Historic Places: February 17, 1987

Short Covered Bridge (Cascadia)
County: Linn, Oregon
Township: Cascadia

GPS Position: 44°23'30.5"N 122°30'36.3"W
Directions: From Cascadia, head SW on US-20 W for 1.3 mi
andturn right onto High Deck Rd to find the bridge
Crosses: South Santiam River
Carries: High Deck Road

Builder: Linn County workforce
Year Built: 1945
Truss Type: Howe
Dimensions: 1 span, 105 feet

Photo Tip: Portal has curve of road and rail in foreground
Notes: The open sides are attractive, especially if you can
find a clear side view

World Index Number: OR/37-22-09#2
National Register of Historic Places: November 29, 1979

Crawfordsville Covered Bridge
County: Linn, Oregon
Township: Crawfordsville

GPS Position: 44°21'24.5"N 122°51'39.3"W
Directions: In Crawfordsville, head west off OR-228 on Courtney Creek Dr and the bridge is a short way
Crosses: Calapoola River
Carries: Courtney Creek Dr
Builder: Linn County workforce
Year Built: 1932 (R1987) (R1996)
Truss Type: Howe
Dimensions: 1 span, 105 feet

Photo Tip: Sides need care but all other views are good
Notes: The bridge was bypassed in 1963 and serves as a pedestrian walkway across the river. The 1996 repairs followed severe flood damage

World Index Number: OR/37-22-15#2
National Register of Historic Places: November 29, 1979

Gallon House Covered Bridge
County: Marion, Oregon
Township: Silverton

GPS Position: 45°01'55.7"N 122°47'53.3"W
Directions: In Silverton, head north on OR-214 N for 0.2 mi and turn left onto Hobart Rd NE. After 0.6 mi turn right onto Gallon House Rd NE where the bridge is 0.5 mi
Crosses: Abiqua Creek
Carries: Gallon House Road
Builder: Not known
Year Built: 1916 (R1965) (R1985) (R1990)
Truss Type: Howe
Dimensions: 1 span, 84 feet
Photo Tip: Good portal view with approaches and treed background
Notes: This is the oldest Oregon covered bridge carrying traffic still. It was badly damaged in a flood in 1964

World Index Number: OR/37-24-01
National Register of Historic Places: November 29, 1979

Stayton-Jordan Covered Bridge
County: Marion, Oregon
Township: Stayton

GPS Position: 44°47'54.8"N 122°47'09.1"W
Directions: 450 N 7th Ave, Stayton
Crosses: Salem Power Canal
Carries: Pedestrian walkway

Builder: Curt Ward
Year Built: 1998
Truss Type: Howe
Dimensions: 1 span, 90 feet

Photo Tip: Easy from all sides
Notes: The original 1988 Covered Bridge burned in a fire in 1994 and the present structure opened in 1998. It services pedestrians moving between islands of Salem Power Canal

World Index Number: OR/37-24-02#2
National Register of Historic Places: Not Listed

Ritner Creek Covered Bridge
County: Polk, Oregon
Township: Pedee-Kings Valley

GPS Position: 44°43'40.4"N 123°26'31.4"W
Directions: From Kings Valley, head east on OR-223 N for 1.5 mi to find the bridge
Crosses: Ritner Creek
Carries: OR-223

Builder: Otis Hamar
Year Built: 1927 (R1976)
Truss Type: Howe
Dimensions: 1 span, 76 feet

Photo Tip: Great side view with fenced approaches
Notes: The bridge was closed in 1976 and moved 60 feet downstream

World Index Number: OR/37-27-01#2
National Register of Historic Places: Not listed

Alva Doc Fourtner Covered Bridge
County: Polk, Oregon
Township: Grand Ronde

GPS Position: 45°04'14.1"N 123°36'59.2"W
Directions: From Grand Ronde, head south on SW Grand Ronde Rd for 0.4 mi and turn right onto A Ackerson Rd. for 0.1 mi
Crosses: South Yamhill River
Carries: Pedestrian Walkway
Builder: Doc and Lydia Fourtner
Year Built: 1932
Truss Type: Queen
Dimensions: 1 span, 66 feet

Photo Tip: All views need careful setups
Notes: The Fourtners built the structure to allow their cattle to cross the river. Private, permission needed

World Index Number: OR/37-27-03
National Register of Historic Places: Not listed

Oregon County Map

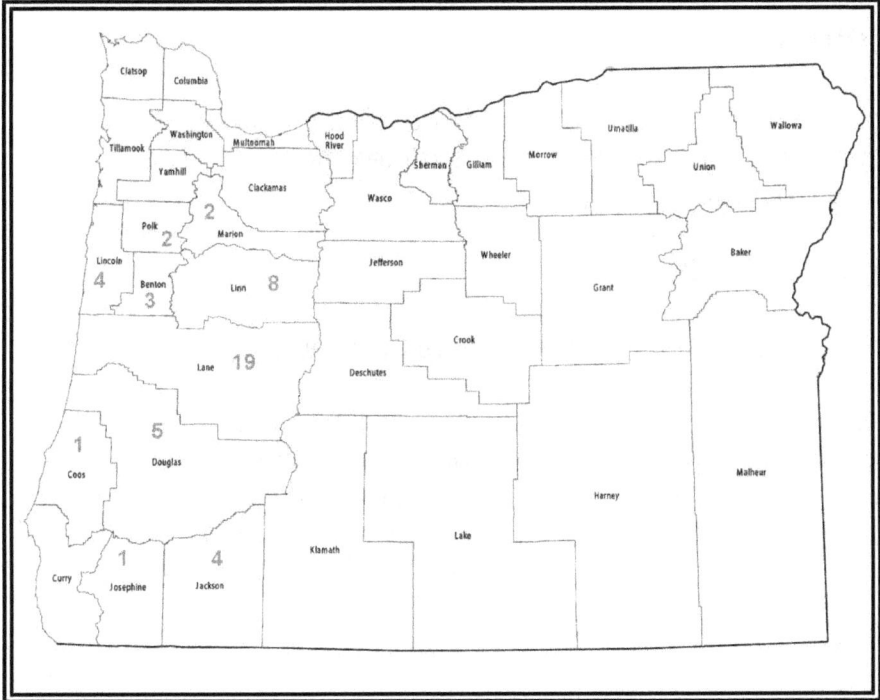

Oregon Tours

The following self-guided tours provide efficient and leisurely day trips to the area bridges. These routes include 75% of Oregon's Covered Bridges

Douglas County Tour

5 Bridges- total driving time is 2 hours 30 minutes

Pass Creek	43°39'38.3"N 123°18'59.7"W
Rochester	43.402062°N 123.363135°W
Cavitt Creek	43°14'38.8"N 123°01'18.4"W
Neal Lane	43°01'01.1"N 123°16'28.3"W
Horse Creek	43°01'24.1"N 123°17'24.1"W

Lane County West Tour

9 Bridges- total driving time is 3 hours 45 minutes

Deadwood Creek	44°08'36.9"N 123°43'13.5"W
Lake Creek	44°06'15.6"N 123°40'25.1"W
Wildcat Creek	44°00'10.9"N 123°39'18.2"W
Coyote Creek	43°58'12.4"N 123°19'08.3"W
Chambers Railroad	43°47'21.7"N 123°04'10.9"W
Centennial	43°47'50.8"N 123°03'51.9"W
Earnest	44°12'05.5"N 122°50'11.3"W
Stewart	43°45'57.6"N 122°59'38.9"W
Goodpasture	44°08'53.0"N 122°35'15.0"W

Lane County East Tour

10 Bridges- total driving time is 3 hours 30 minutes

Dorena	43°44'15.4"N 122°53'01.3"W
Moseby Creek	43°46'41.4"N 123°00'17.3"W
Currin	43°47'34.9"N 122°59'47.3"W
Lowell	43°54'34.5"N 122°46'46.3"W
Office	43°45'30.5"N 122°29'44.6"W
Parvin	43°53'58.1"N 122°49'22.9"W
Unity	43°56'42.5"N 122°46'32.3"W
Pengra	43°57'57.9"N 122°50'42.8"W
Wendling	44°11'28.8"N 122°47'55.6"W
Belknap	44°10'04.9"N 122°13'42.1"W

Lincoln County Tour

4 Bridges- total driving time is 3 hours

Drift Creek	44°59'34.4"N 123°53'15.4"W
Chitwood	44°39'15.2"N 123°49'03.6"W
North Fork Yachats River	44°18'36.0"N 123°58'11.0"W
Fisher School	44°17'29.9"N 123°50'29.0"W

Linn County Tour

8 Bridges- total driving time is 2 hours

Hannah	44°42'43.4"N 122°43'06.3"W
Shimanek	44°42'56.4"N 122°48'15.8"W
Gilkey	44°41'16.3"N 122°54'12.4"W
Hoffman	44°39'12.0"N 122°53'25.5"W
Larwood	44°37'50.4"N 122°44'27.3"W
Crawfordsville	44°21'24.5"N 122°51'39.3"W
Weddle	44°23'40.6"N 122°43'35.8"W
Short	44°23'30.5"N 122°30'36.3"W

Lynch Covered Bridge (Cedar Creek, Grist Mill)
County: Clark, Washington
Township: Woodland

GPS Position: 45°56'18.2"N 122°35'01.0"W
Directions: From the town of Etna, head east on NE Spurrel Rd for 0.8 mi and turn right onto NE Grist Mill Rd where the bridge is a short distance
Crosses: Cedar Creek
Carries: Grist Mill Road
Builder: Not known
Year Built: 1995
Truss Type: Howe
Dimensions: 1 span, 83 feet

Photo Tip: Easy from all sides with an excellent portal view
Notes: The nearby Cedar Creek Grist Mill was restored and this bridge replaced a non-covered bridge as part of the project.

World Index Number: WA/47-06-02
National Register of Historic Places: Not listed

Schafer Farm Covered Bridge
County: Grays Harbor, Washington
Township: Montesano

GPS Position: 47°03'46.8"N 123°31'02.3"W
Directions: From Brady, head north on Middle Satsop Rd for 4.5 mi and take G100 Rd 3.5 mi to Schafer Meadows Lane South where you find the bridge
Crosses: Lagoon
Carries: Schafer Meadows Lane South

Builder: Oscar Hegberg
Year Built: 1966
Truss Type: Howe
Dimensions: 1 span, 72 feet

Photo Tip: Portal are easy but sides need careful setup
Notes: The builder, Oscar Hegberg, used cedar timbers harvested locally. Private

World Index Number: WA/47-14-01
National Register of Historic Places: Not listed

Little Mountain Covered Bridge
County: Klickitat, Washington
Township: Trout Lake

GPS Position: 45°59'29.4"N 121°29'45.7"W
Directions: From the town of Trout Lake, head east on Little Mountain Rd for 1.5 mi and turn left onto Trout Lake Farms Rd where you find the bridge
Crosses: White Salmon River
Carries: Trout Lake Farms Rd
Builder: Not known
Year Built: 1987
Truss Type: Howe
Dimensions: 1 span, 60 feet

Photo Tip: Portal view is best to avoid obstructions
Notes: Moved from Strong Road to here 1987. There is not a lot of information about it

World Index Number: WA/47-20-01
National Register of Historic Places: Not listed

Johnson Covered Bridge
County: Pierce, Washington
Township: Gig Harbor

GPS Position: 47°19'00.6"N 122°38'50.1"W
Directions: From Artondale, head SW on Ray Nash Dr NW for 1.0 mi and turn left onto Whitmore Dr NW. In 0.7 mi turn right onto 67th St NW and the bridge is 0.1 mi
Crosses: Whiskey Creek
Carries: 67th St NW

Builder: Not known
Year Built: 2005
Truss Type: Howe
Dimensions: 1 span, 46 feet

Photo Tip: Open and easy on all sides
Notes: Located on a private drive

World Index Number: WA/47-27-04
National Register of Historic Places: Not listed

Gray's River Covered Bridge
County: Wahkiakum, Washington
Township: Gray's River

GPS Position: 46°21'17.8"N 123°34'52.3"W
Directions: From Gray's River, head east on WA-4 E for 1.4 mi and turn right onto Loop Rd. After 0.2 mi turn left onto Covered Bridge Rd and the bridge is 0.1 mi
Crosses: Gray's River
Carries: Covered Bridge Rd

Builder: Dulin Construction
Year Built: 1989
Truss Type: Howe
Dimensions: 1 span, 158 feet

Photo Tip: Easy from all sides
Notes: The original bridge was opened in 1905. This replacement salvaged some of that bridge

World Index Number: WA/47-35-01#2
National Register of Historic Places: Not listed

Washington County Map

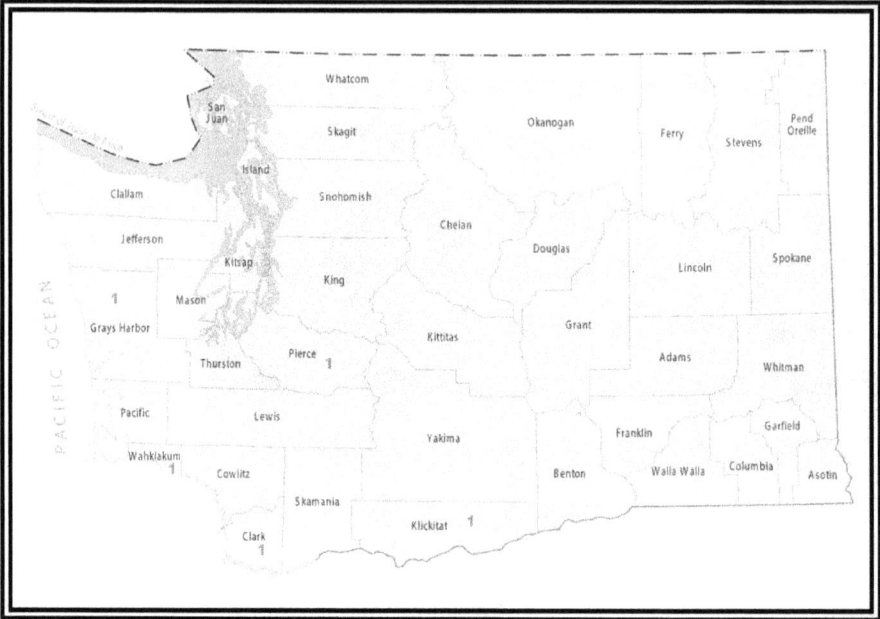

Washington Bridge Tour

Due to the limited number of bridges, spread over a large state, the two northern bridges are not included in this tour. An efficient plan to see the three southern bridges would involve about 3.5 hours of driving as follows:

Little Mountain CB   45°59'29.4"N 121°29'45.7"W
Lynch CB   45°56'18.2"N 122°35'01.0"W
Gray's River CB   46°21'17.8"N 123°34'52.3"W

You can, of course, reverse the order if you prefer to travel west to east.

Glossary

Abutment: The abutments are the bridge supports on each side bank. Usually they were originally constructed of stone but they have often been replaced or supplemented with concrete through the years.

Arch: A curved timber or timber set which is shaped in a curve and functions as a support of the bridge.

Bed timbers: Timbers between the abutment and the truss or bottom chord.

Brace or bracing: A diagonal timber or timber set used to support the trusses.

Bridge Deck: The roadway through the bridge.

Buttress: Wood or metal members on the exterior sides which connect the floor beams and the top of the truss. Used to keep the bridge structure from twisting under wind, water and snow loads.

Camber: A planned curve in the structure to compensate for the weight of the structure.

Chord: The horizontal members extending the length of the truss meant to carry the load to the abutments.

Dead load: The load of the weight of the bridge itself.

Deck: The pathway through the bridge used by pedestrians or vehicles.

Pier: Stone/concrete supports built in the stream bed to support the bridge

Portal: The bridge's entrances.

Post: The truss's vertical members.

Span: The bridge length measured between the abutments.

Treenails or trunnels: Pins or dowels turned from hardwood, driven into holes drilled into the members of the truss to hold them together. Also used in mortised joints.

Truss: The framework which carries the load of the bridge and distributes it to the abutments.

Truss Types

A Truss is a system of ties and struts which are connected to act like a single beam to distribute and carry a load. In covered bridges, these Trusses carry the load to stone abutments at each side and perhaps piers in between. Following are the most common types of Trusses used in Covered Bridges.

Kingpost Truss

Kingpost
Kingpost is the simplest form of Truss with two diagonal members on a bottom chord, often with a vertical post connecting to the diagonals.
The multiple Kingpost involves a series of Kingposts symmetrical from the bridges center. This allows for a much longer span.

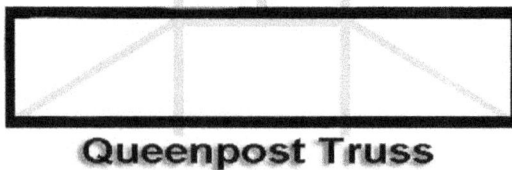

Queenpost Truss

Queenpost
The Queenpost has the peak of the kingpost type replaced with a horizontal top chord which allows for a longer span

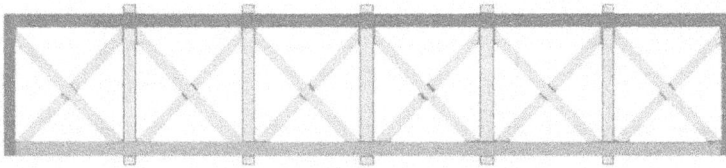

Long

Long

The Long Truss was patented by Stephen Long in 1830. It is a series of X shaped diagonals connected to vertical posts.

Burr Arch

Burr Arch

Invented in 1804 by Theodore Burr, the Burr Arch is one of the most commonly found structures in Covered Bridge design. It is often used in combination with multiple kingposts. The ends of the arch are buried in the abutments.

Howe Truss

Howe

The Howe Truss was patented in 1840 by William Howe. It involves the use of vertical metal rods between the joints of wooden diagonals.

Town Truss

Town

The Town or lattice system was patented by Ithiel Town in 1820. It involved a system of overlapping diagonals in a lattice pattern connected at the intersection by Tree nails or trunnels, wooden pegs or dowels. It had the advantages in that it could be constructed by unskilled labor and local materials could be used.

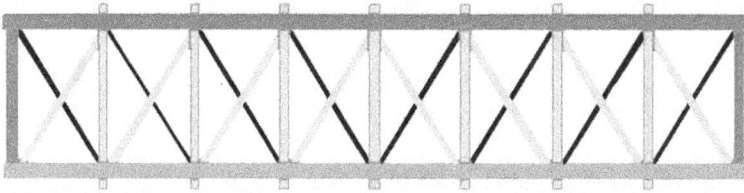

Childs

Childs
The Childs Truss System is essentially a multiple kingpost with half of the diagonal timbers replaced with iron bars.

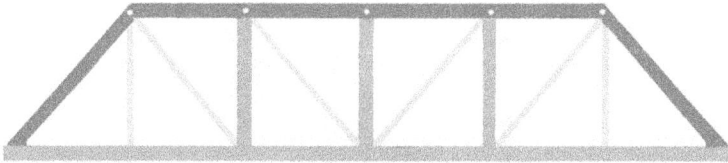

Pratt

Pratt
The Pratt truss was patented in 1844 by Caleb Pratt and his son Thomas Willis Pratt. The design uses vertical members for compression and horizontal members to respond to tension.

Smith Truss

Smith
Robert W. Smith received patents in 1867 and 1869 for variations of his system.

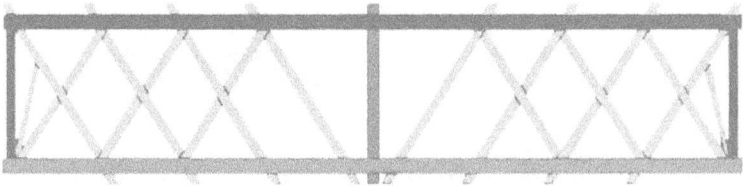

Partridge

Partridge
Reuben L. Partridge received a patent for a design similar to the Smith system but adding terminal braces at the end and a central vertical member.

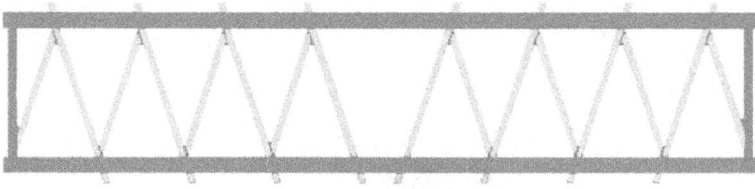

Warren

Warren
Patented in 1848 by two Englishmen, one of whom was named James Warren, it consists of parallel upper and lower chords with diagonal connecting members forming a series of equilateral triangles.

Paddleford

Paddleford
Peter Paddleford worked with the Long Truss system and eventually adapted it with a system of interlocking braces. he was never able to patent the system due to challenges from the owners of the Long Truss patent. However there are a number of New Hampshire and Vermont bridges which use the Paddleford system

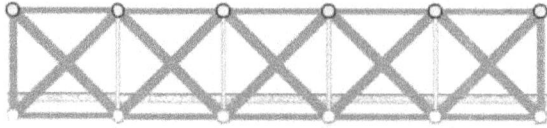

Brown

Brown

Josiah Brown Jr., of Buffalo, New York, patented this system in 1857.It consists of diagonal cross compression members connected to horizontal top and bottom stringers and is known for economic use of materials. It was only used in Michigan where there are a couple of surviving members.

Recently Lost

Hundreds of Oregon Covered Bridges have been lost through the years due to to some of the following causes

- Deterioration through time and use
- Involvement in vehicle accident
- Burned accidentally or otherwise
- Flood or wind damage

The main thing saving these historic structures is the involvement of local concerned citizens

In the last 25 years, two original historic bridges have been lost but happily both have been replaced

Wimer Covered Bridge, Jackson County
Collapsed on July 6, 2003, injuring three people

Oregon Department of Transportation

Replaced in 2008

Chambers Railroad Covered Bridge, Lane County
Demolished in 2011

Oregon Department of Transportation

Replaced in 2011

Manning-Rye CB, Whitman County, Washington
Destroyed in a fire on September 8, 2020

References

National Society for the Preservation of Covered Bridges
http://www.coveredbridgesociety.org

New York State Covered Bridge Society
http://www.nycoveredbridges.org

Vermont Covered Bridge Society
http://www.vermontbridges.com/

Covered Bridge Society of Oregon
http://www.covered-bridges.org/

The Theodore Burr Covered Bridge Society of Pennsylvania
http://www.tbcbspa.com/

Indiana Covered Bridge Society
http://www.indianacrossings.org/

Ohio Historic Bridge Association
http://oldohiobridges.com/ohba/index.htm

Harold Stiver Image Gallery
https://haroldstiver.smugmug.com/Galleries/Themes/Covered-Bridges

Photo Credits:

California
JERRYE AND ROY KLOTZ MD, Powder Works Covered Bridge, **Karora**, Knight's Ferry Covered Bridge

Oregon
Andrew Parodi/Wikipedia CC, Stayton Jordon Covered Bridge, **Akampfer/Wikipedia CC**, Hayden Covered Bridge, **EncMstr/Wikipedia CC,** Office Covered Bridge, **Gary Halvorson, Oregon State Archives**, Coyote Creek Covered Bridge, McKee Covered Bridge. **Katr67/Wikipedia CC**, Fisher School Covered Bridge, **Kirt Edblom/Flickr CC**, Drift Creek Covered Bridge, **Oregon Department of Transportation**, Alva Doc Fourtner Covered Bridge, Chambers Railroad Covered Bridge (original), Wimer Covered Bridge, **Parodygm/Wikipedia CC**, Centennial Coverd Bridge, **Sandy Horvath-Dori/Wikipedia CC**, North Fork Yachats Covered Bridge, Pass Covered Bridge, Ritner Covered Bridge, **Scott Catron/Wikipedia CC**, Harris Covered Bridge, **Sword Fern/Wikipedia CC**, Weddle Covered Bridge, **Visitor7/Wikipedia CC**, Deadwood Creek Covered Bridge, Nelson Mountain Covered Bridge, Wildcat Creek Covered Bridge, **ZabMilenko/Wikipedia CC,** Lost Creek Covered Bridge

Washington
Travisi CC, Gray's River Covered Bridge, **Library of Congress's Prints and Photographs**, Manning Rye Covered Bridge

All other images by the author

The Photographer's and Explorer's Series

Unless noted, there are Print and eBook editions available for the following.

Birding Guide to Orkney
Guide to Photographing Birds

Ontario Lighthouses
Ontario's Old Mills Ontario Waterfalls
Ointario Waterfalls

Alabama Covered Bridges (eBook)
California Covered Bridges (eBook)
Connecticut Covered Bridges (eBook)
Georgia Covered Bridges (eBook)
Indiana Covered Bridges
Maine Covered Bridges (eBook)
Maryland Covered Bridges (eBook)
Massachusetts Covered Bridges (eBook)
Michigan Covered Bridges (eBook)
New England Covered Bridges
Covered Bridges of the Mid-Atlantic
Covered Bridges of the South
New Hampshire Covered Bridges
New York Covered Bridges
Ohio's Covered Bridges
The Covered Bridges of Kentucky (eBook)
The Covered Bridges of Kentucky and Tennessee
The Covered Bridges of Tennessee (eBook)
Vermont's Covered Bridges
The Covered Bridges of Virginia (eBook)
The Covered Bridges of Virginia and West Virginia
Washington Covered Bridges (eBook)
West Coast Covered Bridges
The Covered Bridges of West Virginia (eBook)

Index

Gilkey Covered Bridge	63
Goodpasture Covered Bridge	41
Grave Creek Covered Bridge	37
Hannah Covered Bridge	61
Harris Covered Bridge	24
Hayden Covered Bridge	25
Hoffman Covered Bridge	66
Horse Creek Covered Bridge	32
Irish Bend Covered Bridge	26
Larwood Covered Bridge	65
Lost Creek Covered Bridge	34
Lost Creek Covered Bridge	40
Lowell Covered Bridge	45
McKee Covered Bridge	36
McKenzie River Covered Bridge	42
Moseby Creek Covered Bridge	49
Neal Lane Covered Bridge	31
Nelson Mountain Covered Bridge	40
North Fork Yachats River CB	58
Office Covered Bridge	54
Parvin Covered Bridge	46
Pass Creek Covered Bridge	28
Pengra Covered Bridge	43
Ritner Creek Covered Bridge	71
Rochester Covered Bridge	29
Russell Covered Bridge	51
Sandy Creek Covered Bridge	27
Shimanek Covered Bridge	62
Short Covered Bridge	67
Star Covered Bridge	48
Stayton-Jordan Covered Bridge	70
Stewart Covered Bridge	50
Sunny Valley Covered Bridge	37
Swing Log Covered Bridge	38
Unity Covered Bridge	44
Weddle Covered Bridge	64

Washington

www.ingramcontent.com/pod-product-compliance
Lightning Source LLC
Chambersburg PA
CBHW071102090426
42737CB00013B/2443